RACE OF TRUTH
CAPTAIN SCARLET

Story by Graham Marks
Illustrations by Arkadia
Paper Engineering by Ruth Mawdsley

B☒XTREE

**Designed and manufactured exclusively for Boxtree
by Brown Wells & Jacobs Ltd.**

First published in Great Britain in 1993 by Boxtree Ltd.
Copyright © 1993 ITC Entertainment Group Ltd.
Licensed by Copyright Promotions Ltd.
All rights reserved.

1 3 5 7 9 10 8 6 4 2

Printed and bound in Colombia by Imprepak PUP for
Boxtree Limited
Broadwall House, 21 Broadwall
London SE1 9PL

A CIP catalogue entry for this book is available from the British Library.
ISBN 1 85283 346 7

As darkness fell on the lonely country road, a black-clad figure moved silently through the dense undergrowth that grew almost up to its edge.

Kneeling down, Captain Black, agent of the evil Mysteron empire, quickly assembled the lethal sniper's rifle he was carrying in a small bag. Moments after the job was done he saw headlights in the distance and smiled.

As the sleek limousine approached, Captain Black shot out one of its front tyres and watched as it swerved off the road and crashed into a tree. Packing away his rifle he then started to walk over to the wreck.

Standing by the body of the dead driver, he waited while the strange circles of Mysteron light passed over both the body and the car.

Meanwhile on Cloudbase, the headquarters of Earth's security organisation, Spectrum, the security agency's personnel stopped and listened.

Everywhere in the massive high-tech base, all that could be heard was the weird voice of the Mysterons as it delivered their latest threat to mankind.

"We know you can hear us, Earthmen!" it said. "We have the formula for success, and there's nothing you can do about it!"

"Have you *any* idea what that message meant?" Colonel White asked Captain Scarlet and Captain Blue as soon as they arrived in the Control Room.

"No, Sir," replied Captain Scarlet, "but whatever the Mysterons have done, we're sure to know soon enough!"

Some time later, outside a smart London hotel, a sleek black limousine pulled up. A doorman called into the lobby:

"Doctor Simmons! Your car has arrived to take you to the conference!"

The driver watched, expressionless, as a smartly dressed grey-haired man walked towards him and stepped into the back of the car.

No sooner had the limousine moved off than Captain Black's voice echoed eerily inside it.

"Take him to the rendezvous," he said. "I will be waiting with the truth serum!"

"What's going on!" cried the Doctor, banging on the glass that separated him from the driver. "Let me out of here! I *demand* to be let out!"

"Colonel White!" Lieutenant Green turned from his console. "I've just had a report that a V.I.P. has been kidnapped!"

"Who is it, Lieutenant?" demanded the Colonel.

"It's Doctor Simmons," replied the Lieutenant. "He's the scientist who has invented a formula that allows plants to grow in deserts—he was on his way to a conference to reveal the details to the world press!"

"That must be it!" cried the Colonel. "The formula for success! Get Captains Scarlet and Blue airborne *immediately*—the Doctor can't be far from London, so launch all Angels to give them air cover when they're on the ground in the Spectrum Pursuit Vehicle!"

Moments later a Spectrum jet, piloted by Captain Scarlet, screamed off the Cloudbase airstrip.

Some time later, after picking up the S.P.V., Captain Scarlet contacted the Angels to see if they had spotted anything. High above the English countryside, Destiny Angel, followed in close formation by Harmony and Melody, used their ground radar to track for signs of the hijacked limousine.

Below them, speeding along the winding roads as fast as they could, Captain Scarlet and Captain Blue kept in constant contact with the Angels. Suddenly, through a burst of static, came Destiny's voice:

"I see them, Captain Scarlet!" she said. "They are about a mile ahead of you, and they are approaching a tunnel—that could be their rendezvous!"

"Spectrum Is Green, Destiny" signed off Captain Scarlet. "Adam, you take over the controls—we're going to need split-second timing here!"

Looking through his binoculars, Captain Black could see the headlights of a car coming down the road towards him. Everything was going according to plan. He reached into his pocket and took out a small box containing the truth serum.

The noise of the Angels zooming over him alerted the Mysteron agent to the fact that something might be going wrong. Instead of one set of headlights, he could now see two! Cursing Spectrum under his breath, he disappeared into the undergrowth.

"We've nearly caught up!" said Captain Blue, pushing the S.P.V. to an even greater speed. "What now?"

"Start to overtake, Adam," replied Captain Scarlet, releasing his door catch. "Get as close as you can and watch that he doesn't try and force us off the road!"